Space and Human Culture

Ethics: Space Ethics
Volume 2, Number 1, 2015

Ethics: Contemporary Perspectives
We live in an evolving and increasingly complex global community and with this complexity comes a broad range of ethical issues. The new interdisciplinary journal, Ethics: Contemporary Perspectives, seeks to bring together scholars from across the humanities, social sciences, and sciences, including disciplines as diverse as philosophy, law, medicine and the study of world religions, to discuss these broad ethical issues in contemporary society. A peer reviewed journal, Ethics aimed at exploring our complex world, addressing both old and new ethical issues through scholarly discourse.

This is a new, international, interdisciplinary, and refereed journal which is to be published annually by ATF Press in association with the University of Adelaide Research Unit for the Study of Society, Law and Religion (RUSSLR). The publication is both an on- line and print edition journal. The first issue of the journal has an international line up of leading scholars in a range of disciplines from the USA, Canada, New Zealand, France and Australia. It will address the theme of 'The Ethics of Ethics' and will come out in the first half of 2013. The second edition in 2014 will deal with 'Space Ethics'.

Vol 2/ 1 2015
Subscription rates 2013/2014
Print: Local: Individual $Aus55, Institutions Aus$65.
                        Overseas: Individuals US$60, Institutions US$65.
OnLine: Local: Individuals $Aus $45, Institutions: Aus $55.
                        Overseas: Individuals US$50, Institutions US$60
Print and Online   Local: Individuals $Aus 65, Institutions Aus$85.
                        Overseas: Individuals US$70, Institutions US$80.

Ethics: Contemporary Perspectives is published by ATF Theology and imprint of ATF (Australia) Ltd (ABN 90 116 359 963) and is published once a year.
ISSN 2201-3563

Cover design by Astrid Sengkey. Text Minion Pro Size 11

Space and Human Culture

edited by Jacques Arnould

Adelaide
2015

Vol 2/1 2015

Table of Contents

Vol 2/1 2015

Introduction
Homo Spatiopithecus

Jacques Arnould

There are barely half a thousand people who have left Earth's atmosphere, to cross the theoretical boundary between the Earth and space. Half a thousand astronauts , cosmonauts or astronauts , in their spacecraft beat a path with the American, Russian or Chinese flags. These men and women of space, the first of humanity to belong to the species *Homo spatiopithecus* , all have come back to tell us of their adventures, as extraordinary extra- terrestrial. In 1961, the Soviet leaders Yuri Gagarin asked if he had seen God ; today we ask more willingly to these astronauts how their flight has changed their way of seeing the Earth and predict its future, if their mission was the occasion of a spiritual experience.

Those who, in the late 1950s, decided to develop the areas of space law, came to table for the signing of the Treaty on Principles Governing the Activities of States in the Exploration and Use of Outer space, including the Moon and Other Celestial Bodies, which was signed in December 1966. Then came several other agreements and conventions, and the lawyers and the politicians did not forget Homo spatiopithecus; they even invented a previously unknown concept, that of the 'envoy of humanity'. The more commonly used expression used in diplomatic language, the expression 'sent' was now applied by the Agreement on the Rescue of Astronauts, the Return of Astronauts and the Return of Objects Launched into Outer Space, signed in 1968. It gave the expression a new perspective, as did the astronauts who were the representatives of all humanity. This choice recognised and gave the company of to these astronauts a singular space humanistic dimension. It said that 'the exploration and use of outer space' were 'the province of all humankind' through its most advanced understanding of being sent. These activities can not be the privilege of the few space powers, but should be carried out for the benefit and in the respect of each and every inhabitant of the Earth.

The initiative to introduce these envoys of humankind thus has had a real singularity. Certainly it gives a special status to those who, if they perhaps have some of the kind of 'hero right stuff' (Tom Wolfe) that astronauts and cosmonauts have had in the 1960s, they at least retained an aura of this (at least in the way the public saw them) there was now in addition a clear national recognition. But the legal process is even more remarkable since it gives a form of legal reality to humanity itself. It appears, as a result, as a reflection of the experience of those who are far enough away from Earth to measure the place that our species occupies in the universe. 'We belong to the same planet, we have embarked on the same ship', once perched on the balcony most extraordinary balcony ever offered to Earthlings; 'Take care of it all together', they most often added. Perhaps that is the main message of our report we sent through space travel.

Profoundly humanistic, space law is also in a way declaring outer space part of the common good of humanity. Those who have developed, those who have accepted and signed the successive versions of agreements have thus wanted to show their refusal to reproduce in space the divisions, conflicts which unfortunately have the part of Earthlings. They refused to set boundaries in space whose access must remain free, exploration and exploitation open to all nations for compliance, constraints, obligations and quotas which we know we need to impose. And when they proposed to declare the common heritage of humanity celestial bodies like the Moon, they did not intend to claim, in incredible arrogance, this for humanity, any right of ownership, to be distributed between humans, but rather a common sense of undertaking that would be developed in the coming decades.

Was such humanism utopian in outlook? Yes, in the eyes of those who confuse realism and utopia: in fact, it was impossible in the early 1970s to predict what would be the space activities forty years later. No, for those who recognise in the exercise of utopia, not a projection into the future, but above all a critique of the present. In its own way to give to humankind a common heritage, requiring that all care for future generations, promote cooperation, in short, was everything that was formally introduced into the space law was indeed a real criticism of the conduct of nations then . . . and maybe even ours today ?

Without denying the errors and hypocrisies, the hesitations and failures, space was and still is an extraordinary field of humanisation. That is, in the sense of the precursors of figures such as Vladimir Vernadsky and Pierre Teilhard de Chardin, who had seen in advance or simply perhaps called for the emergence of a noosphere, that is a planetary consciousness. Does not space contribute something in a unique way ? Do not the visions of the Earth that astronauts refer us in space, the images from probes traveling beyond the lunar horizon , but also the networks that now weave multiple satellites around the Earth .contribute something to how we see the Earth and ourselves? Do not all these effects give Homo sapiens an additional quality, and perhaps an essential element, that of spatiopithecus?

Vol 2/1 2015

Human Response to Extraterrestrial Intelligence

Balachandar Baskaran[a], Sissi Enestam[a], Femi Ishola[a],
Dawoon Jung[a], Paul Kelly[a], Dong Weihua[a]
[a] Master of Space Studies Participants - International Space
University, Illkirch-Graffenstaden

Introduction

Humans have long been longing to find an answer to the question: 'Are we alone in this Universe?'

But, what kind of an impact would it bring to our world if this question were answered by being contacted by a technologically advanced extra-terrestrial life? Is the humanity as a whole prepared to meet such a situation in the near future?

This paper attempts to address and analyze the implications and discuss the following actions to be taken of a future postulated scenario in which radio astronomers argue to have received signals from a technologically advanced intelligent extraterrestrial life 100 light years away from Earth. In their message, the extraterrestrial intelligence, ETI, provide their location in the cosmos that astronomers on Earth verify to be correct.

The purpose of this paper is to give an understanding of the immediate and long-term implications from various perspectives involving several disciplines, acknowledging the interdisciplinary nature of the situation. Each section in this paper has been written under guidance, suggestions and opinions obtained from both experts and laymen. The authors of this paper have different backgrounds and come from different places of our planet and together have integrated this interdisciplinary paper bringing forth their experiences and world views . Science and technology, law and policy, culture, religion, ethics, outreach, business, management and economics are the different fields that are discussed in this article. For clarity and coherent flow of topics, the content has been divided into three sections:

Section One: Implications of Receiving an ETI Message.

Section Two: Pros and cons of contacting the ETI.

Section Three: Our Message for the ETI.

The aim of this article is to bring about a debate and discussion within a reader's mind and to enable them to understand the diverse nature of such a situation. We hope that this paper is an analytical and balanced work, and will be useful for people belonging to the space community, policy and decision makers as well as the academics community and can serve as a future reference in case we one day face a comparable situation.

Implications of Receiving an ETI Message

The Authenticity of the Signal

First upon a detection of a signal that could be of alien origin, it is highly important to confirm the detection with multiple telescope observations and to exclude all other possible explanations, such as a hoax originating from Earth. We should also consider the possibility that this may not be an attempt at contact even though it may appear so. We only have to look into our own history to find cultural misunderstandings that had fatal results. If what is a friendly gesture in one culture isn't to another even among humans, how could we expect the same between two interstellar cultures? Perhaps what we consider an attempt at contact is something else completely, such as a radio program transmitted as entertainment. This can be considered to be of relatively low likelihood but should be acknowledged. These cultural differences may pose a threat in further communications with the ETI as well.

Scientific and Technological Considerations

The discovery of an intelligent extraterrestrial civilisation in the galaxy will trigger a domino effect in the human perception and scientific exploration of outer space. At that point, the humanity's place in the universe will be challenged for the first time, providing a hint of the possibility of the spread of life throughout the observable universe. Reception of radio signals from star clusters light years away from our solar system containing specific messages will automatically resolve the Fermi's paradox. It will also reduce the famous Drake equation to particular solutions, and add further strains to the concerns of numerous philosophers, scientists and others about the outcome of an alien contact.

Radio signals in the form of electromagnetic waves travel at the speed of light and given the enormous distances between star systems and galaxies, communication exchange between humans and extraterrestrial communities will require hundreds of years. A signal received from a star system at 100 light years from Earth must have been sent 100 years in the past. This also means that a response to the received message will in turn take 100 years to be received by the ETI. Communication with ETI life will redefine scientific missions and push humans to further advance its technological development. The received ET message providing accurate data of their planet's location might set a new destination for unmanned probes and define their mission approach. Similarly to planetary exploration missions within the solar system, the initial robotic flight to the alien planet should be able to validate the existence of the ETI and characterize the nature of their planet. This could be the human eyes and ears to observe and study the newly discovered world. However, such a mission would take centuries to achieve its objectives with current space transportation technologies. Faster and more efficient interstellar travel technologies will be required to keep the pace with the emerging challenge. Once such a technology has been demonstrated in robotic return missions, a manned voyage to the alien planet might be considered one day when the technology has vastly improved.

It is clearly evident that interstellar communications will play a paramount role in humans' response and reactions to the discovery of the ETI. Low latency and high data rate communication link is desirable for unmanned probes sent to observe the new world. The Voyager spacecraft currently at the edge of the solar system communicates with the Deep Space Network (DSN) with a signal delay of more than ten hours. An unmanned probe at 100 light years away, would communicate with Earth with a delay of roughly one month, neglecting signal attenuation and other perturbations which are significant limiting factors. The question of how will the spacecraft be powered would also need to be answered. Beyond Jupiter, solar panels are obsolete and the common work-horse; Radioisotope Thermoelectric Generator (RTG) outputs depreciates with time. It is unlikely that current RTG technology will be suitable for interstellar missions to 100 light years. Advanced radioisotope power source capable of operating for centuries will have to be developed. Radio Astronomy projects are also very essential. Even with interstellar travel technology, the cosmos is large. Humans do not have to visit every star cluster to study the nature of life in inhabited worlds. With advanced radio astronomy sensors, scientists can make significant studies of the known universe remotely, saving the fear of close contact. Only the waiting time for a response is a problem.

The effects on the humankind would be vast and increased interest in STEM subjects and space sciences in general could be expected to increase. The space industry would be expected to see an enormous increase. Luckily, it is likely that it would also see a large increase in funding partially due to the military applications as will be discussed later in the paper.

Legal and Policy

After the ETI signals have been confirmed by scientists around the world, it will not only have a huge scientific impact, but it will also have implications for the present and future lives of every human being on this planet. Ordinary citizens will want to know how this discovery will impact their everyday lives. Uncertainty and speculation surrounding the true purpose of the ETI message will only grow over time due to the impossibility of real time communication. A growing gap could develop between those who are in control over interpreting the message and implementing policy, and those who are not in control. This could lead to social instability, civil disobedience and international conflict.

Evidence for the existence of other intelligence species in the universe may enhance public enthusiasm for space activities on Earth, and presents an opportunity for all countries to work together to improve space exploration technologies. In this regard, the UN should lead and coordinate outer space contacts and exploration on behalf of the whole planet. Eventually, international cooperation on space exploration may lead to expanded cooperation between states on other issues as well.

Culture, Religion and Ethics

That discovery that life is not unique to Earth will be scrutinized by the world religions. Each religious group will form their official opinion of the discovery and its meanings and effects to their religious views.

The Bible, Qur'an and other religious texts throughout the world describe God's special concern for humanity.[1] Would the discovery of extraterrestrial life then prove that humans no longer occupy a special position in the universe? While some Christian fundamentalists believe that extraterrestrial life would violate the basis of Christian belief, not all share the same view.[2] Some Christians feel that the Bible doesn't exclude the possibility of life outside the Earth, intelligent or not. The Scottish scientist Sir David Brewster argued in 'More Worlds than One: The Creed of the Philosopher and the Hope of the Christian,' that there is no reason why God would have created all the other Suns in the universe if it wasn't to provide heat and light for other worlds. Olson and Tobin add that Sjoerd L Bonting, an Anglican priest and biochemist, thinks that since it is likely that alien life would be composed of similar molecular structures as life on Earth, it is also likely that ETI would have "religious awareness" and could be spiritual creatures. The 14th Dalai Lama once said, "If science proves some belief of Buddhism wrong then Buddhism will have to change," meaning in this context that Buddhism will most likely adapt to the discovery of extraterrestrial life.

The discovery of ETI may also lead to new religions and cults being founded to worship our new acquaintances. There are already a number of 'UFO religions' where the members believe in or worship extraterrestrial beings, one of the most commonly known examples being Scientology.

The spiritual impact of the signal would be seen not only in religious groups but also every individual on Earth. Each person would have

1. Mike Wall, 'Aliens & God: Would Finding Extraterrestrial Life Destroy Religion?', in *Huffington Post*, Retrieved 15 May 2014, http://www.huffingtonpost.com/2012/06/25/aliens-god-extraterrestrial-life-religion_n_1624245.html
2. A Randall Olson and Vladimir VM Tobin, 'An Eastern Orthodox Perspective on Microbial Life on Mars', in *Theology and Science*, 6/4 (2008): 421–437.

an opinion on what this means to their personal worldviews, either agreeing or disagreeing with their religion's point of view or the view of their friends, families and community. This would be something very personal and the signal would bear a very different meaning to each person on Earth. Some could even think of the signal as a divine message; after all when the Spaniards arrived in Mexico the native people regarded them as divine creatures.

Consequently, it is also likely that regardless of the views of different governments, religious groups and international organizations on the matter, contact would be attempted by individuals. It then becomes more important to discuss and prepare for the possible consequences of these contact attempts. Considering that the ETI signal took 100 years to reach Earth, a reply from us will also take a hundred years to reach the ETI. It would therefore be important to send a unified message representing all of humanity with its contents carefully constructed. Such a message should address a few of the most important questions that humankind has for an alien species and those will be discussed in the following sections.

The media would be likely to be producing space documentaries and talk shows explaining the signals and their significance from a various points of view. It would also be likely that the number of fictitious space movies and TV shows and other media products would see a fast increase as fictitious media tends to follow world events closely.

Psychologically, the first contact would likely generate widespread fear, as until the moment of contact, while it was perhaps lonely to be the only known intelligent creatures in the universe, it was safe. This event would mean that while we know we are no longer living in an empty universe, we do not know if it is a safe or a hostile universe that we share.

One easily only concentrates on the rights of humans but forgets to consider to rights of the alien species. The bioethical considerations on alien species have been considered by, for example, William Kramer in his paper 'Colonizing Mars—An Opportunity for Reconsidering Bioethical Standards and Obligations for Future Generations' where he discusses colonizing Mars and the bioethical considerations that may result from finding extraterrestrial life.

The important question becomes, what will stop us from taking advantage of the alien species? It is possible that they are contacting us to ask for help or that by the time we make contact with them again, their situation has changed and they require our assistance. It can be assumed that humanity's answer depends on the request. Through how much trouble would the humans be willing to go through to help strangers of different species? Looking in the history of humankind, if the native people in the conquered countries would had asked for the help of the European conquerors, it seems unlikely that help would had been given. It has been humanities attitude to find new worlds to exploit them, not to offer them help. However, humanitarian organizations such as Red Cross receive vast support in monetary and other forms from people around the world. It might not be too optimistic to assume that the humankind has a empathy for those in a more vulnerable position than themselves. Perhaps our decision on contacting the aliens should include consideration over our own expectations. Are we still interested in cooperation if we are in the giving and not in the receiving end of help and support? Only time itself can answer the question if we have evolved from our fears of the unknown enough to extend these gestures of goodwill and if the 'humanitarian' help will be extended to beings that are not part of humanity.

Business, Management, Economics

Receiving an ETI signal is expected to confer spin-off economic benefits on Earth.[3] These include increase of jobs in SETI-related areas and technology transfer from SETI research to other industries. General interest in space and STEM subjects is also expected to increase.

International cooperation might be expanded. Stock markets could either be negatively impacted by public uncertainty surrounding the message, or speculators could exploit market volatility resulting from such uncertainty. Finally, public budgets for SETI and astrobiology research programs could be expected to increase.

All of these could influence the motives of those directly or indirectly involved in receiving and interpreting the SETI signal;

---

3. Allen Tough, 'Positive consequences of SETI before detection', in Acta Astronautica, 42/10-12 (1998): 745–748.

parties involved may be motivated to not only advocate for increased budgets but also to portray the SETI signal in an advantageous way. SETI scientists could benefit from grants that would expand their research. The defense sector could try to secure increased funding by arguing that the message could be deliberately deceptive, unintentionally misinterpreted or a threat to security in general. As we will see in the discussion of game theory in the section Pros and Cons of , this notion is not entirely without merit.

Informing the Citizens

If many telescopes around the world detected the signal, it is highly likely that the media would hear the news before any decision by the governmental or intergovernmental bodies could be made on how to relay the news to the people. If, however, it was only detected by a large space agency, it is likely that spreading of the news could be controlled for a short while and some control over how to publicize the contact could be exerted. In the past different governments have chosen various approaches on how to relay important news and development to the people but unfortunately more often a partially secretive approach than completely open approach has been taken. In the case of finding life outside Earth, possibly the single most important event in the history of humankind, we believe, that it would be highly recommended to use a completely open policy and further, to begin education programs on what is the significance of the signals especially directed to poor uneducated countries and regions.

The world we live in is highly divided. Not only by geography but even more so by religion, age, wealth and culture. What one person might take as common sense might make no sense at all to another and what beliefs or significance alien contact means to one, can be completely different than what it is to someone else. There is one thing we all have in common, though it may vary in strength between individuals, and that is how we react to things we don't understand; by fear. Fear's greatest enemy is knowledge and therefore to be able to achieve the most rational, educated, approach to these signals and the Extraterrestrial Intelligence, ETI, life is to teach people about the facts. Everyone should form their own opinion based on their cultural background, religion and personality but the more these opinions are based on facts, the easier it is to have meaningful discussions on the subject and to make educated decisions on how to proceed. The extent of negative reactions from the people with regards to subjects such as nanotechnology or genetics could had been largely mitigated if people had been properly informed, in time, on what the technology was really about and its risks and potentials would had been discussed openly. It is therefore suggested that an intergovernmental agency would not only take charge of how to proceed in contacting, or preventing contact with, the aliens but also on educational programs that would be implemented in collaboration with each country. The content of these educational programs could either be based on purely scientific facts to avoid a culturally or religiously biased view. The risk of manipulation of the population would be high, however, and the content of the videos would have to be strictly regulated. This program would face a serious threat of being used to get people to think "the right thing," which in this case would be to share a scientific world view. To avoid any ethical issues, it would be important to ensure that the programs are done together with the leaders and perhaps, humanities, groups in each country to not to violate and cultural or offend any religious beliefs while still factual and informative.

Pros and Cons of Contacting the ETI

Motivations of Contact

The most important aspect of the contact is the motivation of the aliens, in particular, if their intentions are hostile or friendly. This defines what our actions following their contact attempt should be. To study this we start by defining the concept of risk and expand from that to evaluate the risk of contacting the ETI. A risk can be defined in numerous ways, here we will use the definition as given by Kaplan and Garrick.[4] The risk components are the following:

1. A scenario. What could go wrong?
2. A probability. How likely is it to happen?
3. The consequences. If the scenario does happen, what are the consequences?

---

4. Stanley Kaplan and B John Garrick, 'On The Quantitative Definition of Risk', in *Risk Analysis*, 1/1 (1981): 11–27.

We begin by assessing the situation and then deducting the risk factors. The possible motivations for the aliens to attempt to make contact with us, assuming this was a contact attempt, are numerous. First option is scientific which can be further divided in subsections. They may be interested in sharing information with us about the universe and comparing our physiology to learn more about the universe and the life in it. In this case, they should be at a similar technological stage as us for us to have something to offer them. It is also possible that they are at a much later stage in technological and perhaps evolutionary development and they want to help us by providing us technological and scientific advice and information.

It is also possible that they are not interested or willing to share technological information, perhaps due to the danger of affecting a civilizations natural development, but simply want to contact us from curiosity or perhaps there is a large interstellar community they are inviting us to join.

Next we must consider the possibility that their contact attempt has more serious motivations than getting to know one's neighbor or sharing information. Perhaps they want something from us that we are not willing or capable to give. To assess this possibility, one should consider what it is that we could have that they could want. In assuming that the ETI want something physical from us, we must assume that they are capable of traveling at speeds faster than life, or at least at speeds close to speed of life even if they have longer lifespans than humans. This would mean that they are capable of producing or collecting energies that are far beyond the reach of humans. Depending on the propulsion system needed the power requirement varies heavily but an approximation of the energy of the Sun needed for propulsion system is not a too bad approximation. This naturally would imply that the aliens are much further in their technological development than humans and are likely to be a much older civilization. The only exception to this would be if the aliens had gained the skills and knowledge from other civilizations in the universe.

In science fiction aliens often come to Earth to steal our water or other natural resources or in the most apocalyptic ones, to enslave or even consume human beings. Water, is abundant in the universe and we have found it from asteroids, comets, planets and moons. In fact, it would be much more efficient to extract the water from comets than it would be to 'suck' Earth's oceans to a spaceship, after all, all this water would be pulled down quite strongly by Earth's gravity whereas chopping an icy piece of a comet is much more convenient. It can then be said with fair certainty that taking our water would not be a motivation to contact us. For minerals and metals Earth can provide nothing special that can't be found on other astrophysical objects, in fact many minerals are more abundant on other objects and easier to extract than would be, with most imaginable technology, by starting a war with an inhabited planet. It can then be concluded that stealing our natural resources would be a very unlikely motivation to contact Earth. What is left then is life itself. The aliens' need to use humans for consumption is highly unlikely. It is likely that the alien physiology is too different from us for us to be able to provide them with the right nutrients that they require but in addition, humans are not made of anything so unique that cannot be found elsewhere, either from other animals or from other products. Humans themselves can live on carnivorous or vegetarian diet and it is unlikely that even in the likely case that humans and other animals on Earth could provide nutrition to the aliens, that they would want to eat us. Destroying an another intelligent species, especially when one does not need to seems like very unlikely behavior from a species that has evolved enough to learn interstellar travel. While we cannot completely dismiss the possibility that an alien species would be able and willing to use humans, or Earth animals, for nutrition without our consent, we find the risk marginal. If the humans or animals on Earth are not needed for nutrition there is the possibility that they are needed for some other purpose. This is closely related to the unknown unknowns part which for a contact with alien species needs to be acknowledged as an important category. Perhaps the aliens are not biological creatures but artificial intelligence has long ago taken over the biological life on the planet. In that case, perhaps the mechanical life requires some biological constituents that humans and animals on Earth could serve. A risk factor for this is quite impossible to approximate as this and any unknown unknown factor can not be evaluated in the absence of any evidence or data. One can conclude, however, that once again, a civilization, biological or mechanical, that is capable of interstellar travel should be advanced enough to have long ago solved its own problems and its interests and needs would be in other subjects than exploiting other worlds.

For the first and what we consider the most likely motivation of the alien contact, the share of information scenario, the most probable risk factor would be that the aliens were able to share "too much" information with us. In the most extreme situation, the aliens share with us their "encyclopedia" and if they are a much more advanced civilization, this would leave nothing or very little for humans to discover themselves. This could have serious consequences as it could lead to the fall of science and technology studies. Why study something when you can look it up and find the answer? The situation could lead the humankind to a 'cargo cult'. When the steps required to obtain the information would be skipped it is likely that humans would never fully understand the information they were given and would miss important lessons to learn from their mistakes. At worst, humans would not be ready for all the information available and could destroy themselves or even other worlds with the technological applications they are able to create.

The probability for this is quite low however, as first of all, there is no reason to assume that the aliens are that much more advanced than we are and if they are, they can be assumed to know better than to give us information we are not ready for.

For the aliens to want to use humans or other Earth life for selfish and harmful purposes is considered quite a low probability due to the reasons given above, however, if it were to happen, the consequences of it would be dire and would most likely lead to loss of lives.

Science and Technology

Given only the knowledge that the aliens are capable of radio astronomy and giving their own location accurately, almost everything of importance is unknown of them. This includes the level of technological development. It is not only difficult to make assumptions of life outside Earth in general, but it is also very difficult to make assumptions on unknown unknowns such as the technological development of societies. Perhaps radio astronomy, or even the idea of contacting other civilizations is a common phase during the evolution of any society. In that case, every civilization contacted via radio astronomy could be inferred to be at a similar level of technological development. The uncertainties regarding the form of life and level of technological development must be reduced before any decision can be made to send a reply.

Legal and Policy

Before a few scientists or countries rush to make decisions, all states may wish to convene in the United Nations to discuss and reach a legal and political consensus on this event. The SETI Institute has noted that 'many cultures have traditions of depicting strangers, aliens, and ETI, and have different emotional responses to specific terms used within those traditions'.[5] So it can be assumed that it will not be easy for an agreement to be reached where all countries are fully satisfied.

From the government's position, it may be advantageous to answer the ETI rather than to keep silent. This is because if the ETI messages are not answered, uncertainty will remain indefinitely over the motives and potential future actions of the ETI, resulting in potentially negative impacts on the stock market and lingering public dissent as discussed previously. In addition it is highly likely that amateur astronomers, if not prevented, will make contact on their own. In this case, an official message from the humankind might be necessary to prevent any misunderstandings between the humans and the ETI. If a signal is sent back to the ETI then the people will have a chance to know more about the ETI's motives in 200 years time.

Culture, Religion, Ethics

On detecting a signal that could be of alien origin, it is highly important to confirm the detection with multiple telescope observations and to exclude all other possible explanations, such as a hoax originating from Earth. We should also consider the possibility that this may not be an attempt at contact however much it may appear that way. We only have to look into our own history to find cultural misunderstandings that had fatal results. If what is a friendly gesture in one culture isn't to another even among humans, how could we expect the same between two interstellar cultures? Perhaps what we

---

5.   SETI Institute, 'SETI and Human Behavior', Retrieved 8 May 2014 from http://www.seti.org/seti-institute/project/details/seti-and-human-behavior

consider an attempt at contact is something else completely, such as a radio program transmitted as entertainment.

Business, Management, Economics

What about the possibilities of communication as a precursor to interstellar trade or resource exploitation? Population growth and the ever-increasing demand for resources have driven human civilizations to seek out food, land, manpower and energy in increasingly distant territories beyond their own borders. It seems only logical then to extrapolate and imagine economic expansion beyond one's planetary boundaries. Theories on the origin and nature of intelligence suggest that intelligence in general would be socially manipulative, and aggressive towards other species and in terms of expansion of territory.[6] A valuable commodity could very well be a planet to colonize, as the twenty-year search for exoplanets has shown that planets very similar to Earth have so far proven difficult to detect.

However, an important constraint that must be considered is the distance involved. At 100 light years, a starship capable of traveling at 10% the speed of light would take more than 1,900 years to complete a one-way journey including the time needed to accelerate and decelerate.[7] The energy required to power such a ship would be nearly 10^{13} kWh, or approximately 4 times the annual electric energy production of all nuclear power plants on Earth.[8] Clearly the ETI would already need to possess an abundance of energy to power such a trip, and the technology to do so. For an advanced race, such as a Kardashev Type I civilization, this would not be likely to cause a problem as they would already be collecting the entire energy output from their sun.[9] However, resource gathering or trade as a motive for traveling such a distance is clearly problematic as the round trip

6. Douglas Raybeck, 'Predator—Prey Models and Contact Considerations', in *Extraterrestrial Altruism*, edited by Douglas A Vakoch (Berlin/Heidelberg, Springer-Verlag, 2014), 49–63.

7. Using the relativistic rocket equations from http://math.ucr.edu/home/baez/physics/Relativity/SR/rocket.html

8. Assuming a 1000-ton spaceship. Result computed using Wolfram|Alpha. Wolfram Alpha LLC, 2009. Retrieved 11 May 2014 from http://www.wolframalpha.com/input/?i=46400000000000+MJ+in+kWh

9. Nikolai S Kardashev, 'Transmission of Information by Extraterrestrial Civilizations', Soviet Astronomy, 8, 1964.

would at its fastest take 200 years, unless the civilization has a faster than light transportation system. More realistically, however, it can be assumed to take thousands of years. This leaves then the possibilities of exchange of knowledge, curiosity, one-way colonization or military action. Colonization and military action will be considered equal for our purposes as a planet that is already deednsely inhabited such as ours would likely need to be 'emptied' before it can be colonized.

To study the potential strategic impacts of SETI and METI (Messaging to Extraterrestrial Intelligence, or Active SETI), we can use Game Theory. Game Theory tells us that the optimal strategy for an ETI contacting us would be a selfish one,[10] that is, that the ETI would pretend to cooperate with us initially, but betray us. Of course, ETI may choose to communicate for many reasons other than to manipulate us, such as: conducting a census, advertising, curiosity, help, share of information, warning, network establishment, recruitment, jamming, religion, etc.[11] In our case the ETI message received is a 'friendly' one of 'peace', with the intent of soliciting a reply. The earliest manmade radio emissions would only just be reaching the ETI's star systems. Being omnidirectional, these radio emissions will be a faint mixture of incoherent data that would not be a reliable way to understand human civilization. ETI may then have no other means to gather strategic intelligence from us other than by a direct reply. If we do not reply, the ETI may assume that human intelligence does not exist or is not advanced enough. On the other hand, if we do reply then the ETI can confirm our existence. Note that even if our reply is reciprocally altruistic, it does not make a difference to the payoffs; if the ETI wished to maximize its own payoff, then it would be in its own interests to launch a preemptive strike using strategic weapons such as Relativistic Kill Vehicles (RKVs)[12] at less cost than a piloted mission to Earth. The advantages to the ETI

---

10. Mark C Langston, 'The Accidental Altruist: Inferring Altruism from an Extraterrestrial Signal', in *Extraterrestrial Altruism*, edited by Douglas A Vakoch (Berlin/Heidelberg, Springer-Verlag, 2014), 131–140.
11. Jason W Higley, *The SETI Game: Reciprocal Altruism Game Theory Applied to The Search for Extraterrestrial Intelligences (SETI), and Other SETI-related Musings*, third edition, 2013.
12. RKVs are simple, unpiloted projectiles, such as small metallic or rocky bodies, that would be accelerated to a significant fraction of light speed. They would deliver a huge amount of explosive energy on impact. There is no known defense.

would be increased territory and eliminating risk of a similar attack from humans. Disadvantages to the ETI of such a drastic strategy would be loss of a potential ally, retaliation in the case of incomplete destruction, and a large energy expenditure that may cripple their economy depending on their level of technology.

As we have seen, the presence of strategic weapons has the potential to lead to very drastic consequences. We might hope then, that the ETI will consider ethically such decisions. Animal behavior offers some hope: Homes Rolston III notes that when aid is given reciprocally among social animals, the result is increased preservation of the whole group.[13] While intelligent species will still compete with each other, we expect cooperation to emerge as an important interstellar strategy.

Our Message for the ETI

Motivations of Contact

The most important aspect of the contact is the motivation of the aliens, in particular, if their intentions are hostile or friendly. This defines what our actions following their contact attempt should be. To study this we start by defining the concept of risk and expand from that to evaluate the risk of contacting the ETI. A risk can be defined in numerous ways, here we will use the definition as given by Kaplan and Garrick.[14] The risk components are the following:

1. A scenario. What could go wrong?
2. A probability. How likely is it to happen?
3. The consequences. If the scenario does happen, what are the consequences?

We begin by assessing the situation and then deducting the risk factors. The possible motivations for the aliens to attempt to make contact with us, assuming this was a contact attempt, are numerous.

---

13. . Holmes Rolston III. 'Terrestrial and Extraterrestrial Altruism', in Douglas A. Vakoch (ed.), *Extraterrestrial Altruism*. (Berlin/Heidelberg, Springer-Verlag, 2014), 211–222.
14. Stanley Kaplan and B John Garrick, 'On the Quantitative Definition of Risk', in *Risk Analysis*, 1/1 (1981): 11–27.

First option is scientific which can be further divided in subsections. They may be interested in sharing information with us about the universe and comparing our physiology to learn more about the universe and the life in it. In this case, they should be at a similar technological stage as us for us to have something to offer them. It is also possible that they are at a much later stage in technological and perhaps evolutionary development and they want to help us by providing us technological and scientific advice and information.

It is also possible that they are not interested or willing to share technological information, perhaps due to the danger of affecting a civilizations natural development, but simply want to contact us from curiosity or perhaps there is a large interstellar community they are inviting us to join.

Next we must consider the possibility that their contact attempt has more serious motivations than getting to know one's neighbor or sharing information. Perhaps they want something from us that we are not willing or capable to give. To assess this possibility, one should consider what it is that we could have that they could want. In assuming that the ETI want something physical from us, we must assume that they are capable of traveling at speeds faster than life, or at least at speeds close to speed of life even if they have longer lifespans than humans. This would mean that they are capable of producing or collecting energies that are far beyond the reach of humans. Depending on the propulsion system needed the power requirement varies heavily but an approximation of the energy of the Sun needed for propulsion system is not a too bad approximation. This naturally would imply that the aliens are much further in their technological development than humans and are likely to be a much older civilization. The only exception to this would be if the aliens had gained the skills and knowledge from other civilizations in the universe.

In science fiction aliens often come to Earth to steal our water or other natural resources or in the most apocalyptic ones, to enslave or even consume human beings. Water, is abundant in the universe and we have found it from asteroids, comets, planets and moons. In fact, it would be much more efficient to extract the water from comets than it would be to 'suck' Earth's oceans to a spaceship, after all, all this water would be pulled down quite strongly by Earth's gravity whereas chopping an icy piece of a comet is much more convenient. It can then be said with fair certainty that taking our water would not be a motivation to contact us. For minerals and metals Earth can provide nothing special that can't be found on other astrophysical objects, in fact many minerals are more abundant on other objects and easier to extract than would be, with most imaginable technology, by starting a war with an inhabited planet. It can then be concluded that stealing our natural resources would be a very unlikely motivation to contact Earth. What is left then is life itself. The aliens' need to use humans for consumption is highly unlikely. It is likely that the alien physiology is too different from us for us to be able to provide them with the right nutrients that they require but in addition, humans are not made of anything so unique that cannot be found elsewhere, either from other animals or from other products. Humans themselves can live on carnivorous or vegetarian diet and it is unlikely that even in the likely case that humans and other animals on Earth could provide nutrition to the aliens, that they would want to eat us. Destroying another intelligent species, especially when one does not need to seems like very unlikely behavior from a species that has evolved enough to learn interstellar travel. While we cannot completely dismiss the possibility that an alien species would be able and willing to use humans, or Earth animals, for nutrition without our consent, we find the risk marginal. If the humans or animals on Earth are not needed for nutrition there is the possibility that they are needed for some other purpose. This is closely related to the unknown unknowns part which for a contact with alien species needs to be acknowledged as an important category. Perhaps the aliens are not biological creatures but artificial intelligence has long ago taken over the biological life on the planet. In that case, perhaps the mechanical life requires some biological constituents that humans and animals on Earth could serve. A risk factor for this is quite impossible to approximate as this and any unknown unknown factor cannot be evaluated in the absence of any evidence or data. One can conclude, however, that once again, a civilization, biological or mechanical, that is capable of interstellar travel should be advanced enough to have long ago solved its own problems and its interests and needs would be in other subjects than exploiting other worlds.

For the first and what we consider the most likely motivation of the alien contact, the share of information scenario, the most probable risk factor would be that the aliens were able to share 'too much' information with us. In the most extreme situation, the aliens share with us their 'encyclopedia' and if they are a much more advanced civilization, this would leave nothing or very little for humans to discover themselves. This could have serious consequences as it could lead to the fall of science and technology studies. Why study something when you can look it up and find the answer? The situation could lead the humankind to a 'cargo cult'. When the steps required to obtain the information would be skipped it is likely that humans would never fully understand the information they were given and would miss important lessons to learn from their mistakes. At worst, humans would not be ready for all the information available and could destroy themselves or even other worlds with the technological applications they are able to create.

The probability for this is quite low however, as first of all, there is no reason to assume that the aliens are that much more advanced than we are and if they are, they can be assumed to know better than to give us information we are not ready for.

For the aliens to want to use humans or other Earth life for selfish and harmful purposes would lead to dire consequences and most likely to loss of lives.

Legal and Policy

During the wait between our reply to the ETI and their response, governments are likely to go through three different periods: Heating, Cooling and Waiting Periods.

The Heating Period describes the interval between the ETI messages being received, to all states beginning to discuss how to react. This will be a dangerous time with many variables involved. Different people will have totally different reactions; excitement from within the scientific community, and extreme reactions from some religious and other groups can be anticipated. For the international community, the first and most important task is to make sure that no individual, group or country will send signals back to the ETI, independently, before a consensus is reached. Censorship of the whole ETI message is probably not feasible as private enthusiasts could also access the signals. In addition, openness may prevent many problems in the following stages and would mitigate fear among the people and feelings of mistrust towards the government. However, the key technical details regarding the message and the coding required for a reply could be withheld until all states can agree on a unified policy. While this approach would likely be necessary, it is worth noting that taking an individual's right to communicate with the ETI is a violation of personal freedom and the decision should not be made lightly.

The Cooling Period describes the interval between discussion within the United Nations (UN), to send an answer to the ETI. This will be a time when emotions transition to rational decisions. Political leaders will have discussed the issue thoroughly and decided on a policy. However, certain aspects of this policy will only be implemented hundreds of years in the future. The persons who made the policy will no longer be present in such a distant future. So care must be taken to adopt a consensus that is accepted by the whole international community. A UN convention describing the agreed policy in legal terms should be ratified. The following might describe the underlying principles of such a convention:

1. Messages from ETI present opportunities for improvements in science as well as global cooperation;
2. The UN will represent Earth in all contacts with the ETI, and the UN will have the sole right to contact the ETI and in a peaceful manner;
3. Every message from the ETI will be shared with all states.

The Waiting Period will be the longest and hardest time for everyone. Governments will have to prepare for public expectation to 200 years later. Though the situation is quite unique and not completely comparable, some analogs for this exist; for example, fears that surrounded the Y2K bug and the 2012 'Mayan' prophecy. Options available for policymakers in preparing for a negative sentiment might include engaging religious groups in outreach activities, and encouraging the media and artists to create positive works to help people understand and deal with this issue. It would also be very important to educate the general people of the signal, extraterrestrial life and the implications of the signal as in the end, knowledge, is the best weapon against fear.

Business, Management, Economics

It would be prudent for Earth to analyze very carefully the messages that the ETI sent, in order to estimate to the best approximation possible, the ETI's level of technological and social development, as well as to determine the accuracy of the messages by optical telescope observations. If duplicity is suspected, then the best strategy for humans is to not reply at all. If the content of the message is verified, then a cautious reply from us should be considered. The content of such a reply should use abstract means such as music to convey kinship and altruism. Images or information regarding the biology of humans should be avoided.[15]

Conclusion

The most fundamental aspect after an ETI communication is confirming the authenticity of such a signal in the most effective and rapid way possible. This is very important since it will avoid undue societal complications and disturbances. The second most important part would be to interpret the message. Communication varies with culture, time and location. Hence, it is absolutely essential to evaluate such a signal and make sure we know what have been communicated to us. The smallest of uncertainty necessarily would stop us from have a direct influence on our decision to respond to their signals. At the same time, it'll also help us in creating a perception about the communication that could either be positive or negative.

Confirmation of the existence of ETI would prove the fact that we are not alone in this universe. This in turn would increase the quest for the search of more life across the universe. New technologies will be developed in the fields of radio communication as well as interstellar travel. From a safety point of view, technological advancements in defense will be made. There will be numerous spin offs from these developments that will have positive effects on economies.

The UN and international organizations will undoubtedly play a major role under such scenarios, to bring about clarity with respect to ETI, their communication, and response to such a signal and to bring

---

15. Jerome H Barkow. 'Eliciting Altruism while Avoiding Xenophobia: A Thought Experiment', in Douglas A Vakoch (ed.), *Extraterrestrial Altruism*. Berlin/ Heidelberg, Springer-Verlag, 2014, p.37–48.

about a balance in economy in case there's a downfall. Short and long term goals and policies related to them will also be created.

There will be both positive and negative impacts in the global economy. Certain areas such as defense, science and technology may be boosted but at the same time it is natural that that there will be fluctuations among global markets increasingly because of fear which leads to uncertainties.

Different religions will have different viewpoints over this but certainly will take a stand over time, whether positive or negative, only time can tell. But, it shall surely have influence among people. Apart from these, individual decisions and evaluation will play a major role in the context of the situation and near future. There is no doubt that there will be fear among people over ETI. There will be an abundance of communication and discourse that would happen as a resultant of these. Apart from science fiction gaining popularity among adults and kids, the education system will debate the pros and cons of ETI contact. New fields of study might also emerge from these developments.

One of the biggest factors which is both an advantage as well as a disadvantage to humans is the time and space in between us. To establish a communication it takes a century, and to get a response, it takes twice that time. The increase in time creates internal chaos but also gives us enough time to prepare in case of an invasion. It is essential that the response to such communication be cautiously approached and any information regarding the biology of humans and living creatures aren't exposed. When positively approached, time and space will be the biggest limiting factor in case there is an establishment of trade between the two planets. New types of transportation beyond existing boundaries could only pave way for a future betterment of both civilizations.

At the end, though both ETI and humans will be cautious in their approach, it is evident that negative perceptions and positions will bring destructions to both the planets. A positive approach will help both in moving forward to co-exist, collectively grow and in finding more life across the vast expanse of the Universe.

Space Seen From Rome[1]

September 1956: the city of Rome hosted the seventh Congress of the International Astronautic Federation, and offers speaking time to Pope Pius XII, its delegate. It is probably one of the very first times that a pope has officially made a speech about one of humanity's major achievements in the course of the twentieth century, but which at that time was still taking its first faltering steps: the conquest of Space. 'We speak Our admiration of the conviction, tenacity, audacity of all those who, for half a century, step by step, have been conquering this immense domain, Space', Pius XII began. Half a century, since it was in 1926, the pope recalled, that the first liquid fuel rocket was launched in the United States. The pope did not forget the strategic use of rockets, inaugurated during the Second World War by V1 and V2,[2] but above all he held to the intellectual development demanded or stimulated by space activities:

> If up to the present mankind has been feeling shut in on earth, as it were, and has had to be content with the fragments of information that reach him from the universe, it now seems that he is offered the possibility of breaking that barrier and having access to new truths and new knowledge.

Knowledge about humanity itself, but also about the world and about God: 'It's the whole creation', Pius XII made clear, 'that [God] has

---

1. Jacques Arnould, *God, the Moon and the Astronaut: Space Conquest and Theology* (Adelaide: ATF Press, 2016), 67-96.
2. I mean the modern military use of rockets: the Chinese used them in the tenth century of our era, St Louis to defend the town of Damiette in Egypt in 1249, St Joan of Arc in 1429 to deliver Orleans, and the Turks to besiege Constantinople in 1453!

entrusted to him and that he offers to the human spirit so that he may penetrate it and can therefore understand ever more deeply the infinite grandeur of his Creator'. In any case, this effort of humanity, in depending on all the resources of science and modern techniques, should always arise from international collaboration, with the concern that this work can be profitable to humanity: this peaceful conquest of the universe 'must contribute to impressing more strongly on the conscience of men the sense of community and solidarity, so that all have more of an impression of being part of the great family of God, of being children of the same Father'. To put it another way, 'the most daring explorations of space will serve only to introduce a new ferment of division if they are not balanced by deeper moral reflection and a more conscious attitude of devotion to humanity's higher interests'.

A few years later, Pope John XXIII ascribed to the same state of mind with regard to space. On the 16th May 1963, while the American Gordon Cooper was accomplishing his twenty two revolutions around Earth on board the capsule Mercury, good Pope John, in the course of a speech addressed to the Council General of Pontifical Missionary Works, in his commentary on the encyclical Pacem in terris, evoked this new stage in space conquest: 'We accompany with Our prayers and Our blessing the space exploits that are being renewed and perfected. We wish them the real success that contributes to brotherhood and to civilisation.' He concluded with this exhortation: 'Let us remain at our tasks which transcend all heights, all speeds and all technical triumphs, let us try decisively and confidently to approach the man of God and cause the fervour of the holy Gospel to penetrate social life.'

The same tone with Paul VI: on the occasion of the Feast of Pentecost 1965, he prolonged the prayer to the Virgin (Regina Coeli) with an intention destined for the American astronauts White and McDivitt, on board Gemini IV: 'May Our Blessing reach the whole earth and even mount into the sky for those who, at this very time, are exploring new astral paths.' A few weeks later, at Castel Gandalfo, during the Angelus of the 29th of August, he said he had 'a special thought for the two astronauts who are finishing their space flight right now. While wishing that with God's protection, they can bring their wonderful, heroic exploit to a good end, [We contemplate] with admiration the steady and unimaginable progress of science and technology'. It was a question of the Americans Cooper and Conrad who were in the process of beating the record for the length of time in space, in the course of the Gemini V mission. One year later, it was from the balcony of the Vatican that he invited prayer for Stafford and Cernan, another two American astronauts, 'these pioneers of the conquest of celestial space, these most daring representatives of the power given by science, technology and modern human research'.

On the 23rd December 1969, before the Sacred College and the Roman Curia, gathered on the occasion of Christmas good wishes, Paul VI paid homage 'to the genius, action, courage of the men who apply themselves to this kind of conquest', and formulated 'best wishes for the good, fruitful success of their wise, daring enterprises', and implored 'God's help for the astronauts, for all their collaborators, for humanity watching and reflecting'. For the first time men were in the process of travelling around the Moon. At the time of the general audience of the 21st May 1969, he meditated for a long time on the Apollo X mission, during which the lunar module approached the lunar surface, with Stafford and Cernan on board. On the 21st of July 1969, Armstrong then Aldrin brushed the lunar surface, while Collins, the third member of the Apollo XI mission, did a solitary revolution around the moon. On the 16th of October of that year, Paul VI received the three astronauts in a private audience. He told them of his admiration for their courage and the spirit with which they fulfilled their mission: that of peace and service for humanity; he recalled how his prayers and those of the Church went with them, and he congratulated them and all those who contributed to the bringing about of this enterprise. The Apollo XIII events were evoked on the occasion of the Twelfth Week of Study of the Pontifical Academy of Science, in the pope's speech of the 18th April 1970, and the Angelus of Sunday the 7th February 1971 again gave the occasion to evoke 'the extraordinary lunar vehicle' of the Apollo XIV mission.

In June 1971, while the Americans were travelling over the moon's surface on board an electric buggy, three Soviet cosmonauts, Dobrovolski, Patsayev and Volkov, met their deaths in the Soyuz II accident, at the moment of re-entering earth's atmosphere. On the 30th of June, Paul VI, while inaugurating the new audience hall of the Holy See, evoked the grief caused in him by 'this tragic and unexpected epilogue to their enterprise, which had aroused so much admiration and of which the sad end heightens still more the risk which they ran and their heroism.'

Subsequently, even if, on the 4th of November 1998, John Paul II accepted a space suit given by six Russian cosmonauts who had come to Rome to take part in a conference on ageing, the pontifical interest was more centred on the philosophical and ethical dimensions of the space enterprise.[3]

Thus, still in the course of the general audience of the 21st May 1968, Paul VI broadened his reflection beyond the technological exploit:

> And, as if a window were opening in our daily life, here we are, being invited to look out, into space, into the sky, into the cosmos. And, as it is a question of a human phenomenon which has the sky as its setting, our usual thoughts are as it were grabbed by the emptiness that opens before us. Our first reaction is not of wonder but of being disturbed. Before us there opens a reality that is immense and mysterious and that we thought we could forget about, because for us who are not astronomers, it was distant, inaccessible and beyond our experience. Our vision plunges into the depth of space; its field extends beyond measure; at least, the universe is telling us that it exists. On certain beautiful summer nights, we too have perhaps contemplated the numberless stars which are scattered over the immense vault of the heavens; we have thought, or have tried to think, of the mystery of the universe. Perhaps, before this wonderful, mysterious external vision, we have internally heard the melancholy tune which Leopardi's shepherd sang while wandering in the night in solitary Asian places. Perhaps the feeling for the infinite, which may transcend the infinite and time, has given to us too a metaphysical trembling before this ocean of the being in which our life is plunged; and yet, this, as little as it may be, is life, conscience, spirit.

---

3.   On the 2nd May 2001, *Le Canard enchaine* mentioned a diplomatic incident between the Vatican and NASA: 'The American space agency has refused permission for Umberto Guidoni, an Italian astronaut, to transmit a message from the Pope from the ISS (International Space Station). NASA is afraid that such an initiative might offend other religions.'

Less than twenty years beforehand, Pius XII became enthusiastic over the results of modern astronomy, to the point of lapsing into a kind of 'concordism'. God would await us, he said, behind each door opened by science.[4] Certainly, in his speech of 1968, Paul VI did not follow in the steps of his predecessor; but even so he spoke of this 'contact with a veil behind which is felt the breath of an infinite presence' (as, at the time of the Angelus on 29th of December 1968, on the return of Apollo VIII of 'the necessity of the idea of God, of his existence and of knowing Him [which] is imposed with more strength'). He continued: 'That elbows aside the small-minded and empirical idea that we often make for ourselves of God; it broadens to infinite our childish thinking and urges it to say the Gospel prayer again, giving it new, deep meaning: Our Father who is in Heaven'. A few months later he again said: 'If this cosmos exists, and if it appears to us on the one hand so laden with mystery (science tells us so, especially mathematics and physics; the movements, forces and laws . . . that we are discovering in it confirm it), and on the other hand, one could say, so impregnated with a thinking not its own, but infused, reflected, operating, and decipherable, knowable, put at our disposition, that means that this cosmos is unrolling from a transcendent principle, a creative thinking, a secret, superior power . . . that is to say, that it has been created' (16th July 1969). The discovery and observation of the cosmos would be 'a modest but always great catechism lesson', inviting us to 'see God in the world, and the world in God'.

'What man is capable of such great things?' Paul VI wondered again on 20 July 1969. Like a vision of God, that of man aroused in the popes by the space enterprise is marked by 'metaphysical trembling'. Fear and admiration: so it's not by chance that Paul VI entrusted Psalm 8 to the astronauts of *Apollo XI*. In the technological and scientific adventure which was begun in 1957 and was in full flight in the 1960s, each day the microcosmic reality of humanity was revealed more; however, its smallness did not prevent it from possessing extraordinary capacities for intelligence and inventiveness, adaptation and conquest. 'Man' said Paul VI on the 7th of February 1971,

---

4. Jacques Arnould, *Dieu, le singe le big bang . Quelques défis lancés aux chrétiens par la science* (Paris, Éditions du Cerf, 2000), 85 ff.

this atom of the universe, what is he not capable of! Honour to man, to thought, to science, to technology, to work, to human boldness. Honour to the synthesis which man has been able to make between science and its application, he who, differently from all other animals, can give the means of conquest to his intelligence and his hands. Honour to man, king of the earth and now prince of the heavens. Honour to the living being that we are, reflecting in himself the face of God and who, by dominating things is obeying the biblical command: fill the earth and subdue it . For centuries, man has been reflecting on his enigma: know yourself. Today he is progressing into that self-knowledge. He is a fruitful bough, as the Bible says (Gen 49:22). Man sees reflected in himself his invisible mystery, the immortal spirit, and he obeys his natural destiny which pushes him to make progress. There it is not a question of vain ambition, but a response to the vocation of his being, which at the same time is learning to read in the cosmos the compulsion of a creative principal that is mysterious and silent, eternal and all powerful, and which thinks and acts.[5]

This last quotation underlines how, without ignoring the limits or excesses of the space enterprise, the tone of the pontifical speeches on man is above all admiration, that of Psalm 8, or again that of the injunction from the Book of Genesis: 'Fill the world and subdue it'. Pius XII has already made a reference to it:

The Lord God, who placed in the heart of man the insatiable desire to know, did not intend to set a limit on his efforts at conquest, when he said: Subdue the earth. It was the whole creation that he entrusted to him and which he offered to the human spirit, so that he might penetrate it and might thus understand ever more deeply the infinite grandeur of his Creator (20 September 1956).

---

5. At the end of the nineteenth century, Father Ortolan was already writing: 'Yes! Progress in astronomy by itself could reveal to man his power and grandeur! The other inventions of his fertile genius were incapable of giving him such a lofty idea of his soul (Astronomie *et Théologie,* [Paris-Lyon, Delhomme et Briguet, 1894] 10). Note that Flammarion is considered by Ortolan as 'one of those romantics of astronomy' and that the ecclesiastic defends the idea of the fixedness of species (proven by memorable experiments!).

This constant returning to the confession of God the creator, with which every creature maintains a relationship of dependence, is written into the continuing elaboration, all through the pontifical discourses of the second half of the twentieth century, of what John-Paul II called a new humanism. In other words, of a thinking 'in which the spiritual, moral, philosophical, aesthetic and scientific values are developed in harmony, and in which liberty and the rights of the human person are deeply respected [. . .] for the spiritual and material well-being of all humanity' (7 November 1986), which is not without demanding some ethical type constraints.

On the 9th of August 1982, addressing the Second Conference of the United Nations on the exploration and peaceful use of extra-atmospheric space, Monsignor Mario Peressin chose to evoke an objection currently made with regard to the space enterprise:

> After all, is there not rather excessive enthusiasm involved in it? Would the conquest of space not lead the most powerful States and the scientific community to forget our fundamental human problems (the drama of poverty and hunger for hundreds of millions of human beings, the scourge of strikes, which is spreading more and more in industrial society, without forgetting chronic under-employment in poor countries, etc? Should we not strive first to resolve these dramatic problems? Would the conquest of space not be a costly, useless luxury, as well as a dangerous diversion?

Monsignor Peressin gave direct answers to these questions: 'It is essential to pursue it, in the very interest of humanity.' This interest is not only practical (the prelate did not fail to enumerate the different applications of space technologies, in particular in the areas of telecommunication, meteorology or remote detection); he is also into the value of example possessed by the space enterprise. What should we understand by that?

In the eyes of Rome and as the preceding quotations have abundantly illustrated, the contemplation and exploration of the cosmos have had, and still have, a positive influence on man's self-understanding. The space enterprise can even serve as an example, Paul VI recalled, the day following the success of the Apollo XI mission, in particular for young people subject to the pull of today's fashionable defeatism with regard to society and modern life in general [. . .] Life, on the contrary, is serious, as everything that a colossal space enterprise shows us in what it takes for granted in the way of study, defence, labour, planning, attempts, risks, sacrifices. It is easy to criticise, to debate; less so to be constructive; in the case We are speaking of, certainly, but also in the very numerous others that our present civilisation offers us. That is why it seems to Us that the event which we are celebrating gives us a duty to reconsider and appreciate the values of modern life. We do not deny the right to criticise, We do not reproach young people for their instinct for emancipation and novelty. But we consider that the iconoclastic, debased degrading of love revealed by professional proponents is not worthy of the young. The young ought to experience the ideal, the positive to which the magnificent space adventure calls them.

And the popes have not ceased to highlight or to call attention to the peaceful nature of the space enterprise. 'This common effort of all humanity for a peaceful conquest of the universe' said Pius XII as early as 1956, must contribute to impressing more into men's awareness the meaning of community and solidarity." 'May the coming year', John XXIII also said on the occasion of Christmas greetings 1962,

record many more of these peaceful conquests due to man's genius! And may God be willing to inspire in the organisers of these great space enterprises the idea of involving in their efforts and their experiments capable, daring men from every nation and every race. In that way they will have worked effectively for brotherhood and peace which are the object of the greetings and prayers of all in these holy days of the festival of Christmas.

A similar wish in the mouth of Paul VI at the time of the first extra-vehicular walk in history, accomplished by the soviet cosmonaut Leonov, on board Voskhod II, in March 1965: 'With all Our soul, We shall formulate this wish: that all this progress may serve to make men better, more united and more determined to serve the ideals of peace and the well-being of all.' The same at the time of the mission of Gemini V ('We hope that [these conquests] will always strive towards the peace, wellbeing and harmony of humanity') or again at the time of the launch of the American Early Bird communication satellite, on the third of May, 1965:

> We pray the all-powerful God that these wonderful discoveries may serve the cause of peace and permit men to cooperate all together by making this world a better and happier place where man may develop in the image of his Creator and find the realisation of his desires, to the extent that that is possible on earth.

Finally, John-Paul II, on the 20th June 1986, before a group of the Pontifical Academy of Science, meeting around the theme of the impact of remote detection by satellite on the economy of developing countries, expressed the wish 'that with the aid of common accords and undertakings all governments may promote the peaceful use of space resources, in the quest for the unifying of the human family in justice and peace'. The pope recognised that certain space enterprises possessed of themselves 'the meaning of peace and harmony', like those directed towards Halley's comet, and of which he received those in charge in December of the same year; but he assessed, doubtless better than his predecessors, how much the use of space can equally turn out to be contrary to vows of peace, solidarity and fraternity.

Paul VI, of course, was not ignorant of the spirit of competition which prevailed over the space enterprises: shortly before the launch of the Italian satellite San Marco II, in May 1965, he evoked the 'peaceful and uplifting competition for the conquest of space'. And in August 1964, when the American probe Ranger VII had just put down on the surface of the moon, he prayed 'that in this progressive conquest of the world, of nature and of knowledge of it, man may not go astray, may not become boastful' or again 'may not yield to the materialist temptation that this progress may bring, but may know how to see in it new motivation to understand in it the graces received from God that have elevated us to the spiritual order'. The peaceful potential of the space ideal, like its fragility, did not therefore escape John XXIII and especially not Paul VI; but they remain above all influenced by the admiration aroused by astronautic achievements and the progress that has thus become apparent. John-Paul II, without denying the usefulness of space activities, puts the accent rather on the questioning , indeed the ethical urgency that these activities call forth; they arise from a necessity. 'Modern space technology', warns John-Paul II before the Pontifical Academy of Science, on the 2nd of October 1984, 'must not be employed to sustain any cultural imperialism to the detriment of the authentic culture of human beings with the legitimate differences that have developed in the history of each people'. A few themes particularly hold his attention: militarization and national sovereignty, natural resources and ecology, and intercultural matters.

The use of space for military ends is absolutely contrary to the stipulations of the 'Treaty on the principles governing the States in the matter of exploration and utilisation of extra-atmospheric space, including the Moon and the other celestial bodies' (1967); this treaty even details, in its third article, that 'the States party to the Treaty undertake not to put into orbit around the Earth any object bearing nuclear weapons or any other type of weapons of mass destruction, not to install such weapons on celestial bodies, and not to place such weapons of any other kind, in extra-atmospheric space'. By such interdictions, Monsignor Peressin emphasises, in his speech of 9th August 1982, international law takes on a whole planet orientation, in other words becomes that of all humanity. This orientation is not without its echoes in the constitution of the Second Vatican Council Gaudium et spes: 'God has destined Earth and all that it contains for the use of all men and all peoples in order that the good gifts of creation may flow equitably through everyone's fingers, according to the rule of justice, which is inseparable from charity' (No 69, # 1). And in fact, as John-Paul II underlined in 1984, with the knowledge and practice of modern technology,

> it would be possible to create programs suitable to help the world to conquer the lack of balance in agricultural practice, the advance of deserts, and ecological disasters provoked by human greed with regard to the earth, in water systems and the atmosphere, with the ever more alarming destruction of animal and vegetable life, and with serious and fatal illnesses which affect human life itself.

The sharing of resources, cooperation, fraternity: the space milieu but above all the speeches that are inspired by its achievements, including speeches of the popes, have made use of and do willingly use these words. But no one is deceived: when the phase of research, trial and fine tuning come to an end, and when programs enter into the operational phase, fine intentions often have a tendency to evaporate, fears to be expressed, and personal interests to reappear. For example that is the case in the controversies aroused by the threat that space technology causes to hang over national sovereignty, in particular those of remote detection (over flying and observation of territory) and telecommunication (the possibility of 'breaking into' the cultural network of a country without being harassed. Monsignor Peressin evoked this difficulty:

> Two principles must be taken into consideration at the same time: firstly that each State enjoys legitimate independence and has the right to act freely, all the while respecting the rights of others and on the basis of universal inter-human solidarity; and next, that sovereignty is not an absolute right, and that it may notably forbid free cultural exchanges, for it must also be situated in the same basis of universal inter-human solidarity.

That is one way of recalling that techno-scientific progress must of necessity be accompanied not only by ethical effort, but, more than that, by an evolution in attitudes of mind and cultures.

Beside the theological, philosophical and ethical nuances of the pontifical speeches, other religious voices are raised which maintain a more conquering tone.

The Chapel on the Moon

Turin, October 1997. The old Fiat car factory, transformed into a conference centre, that year welcomed participants to the 48th congress of the International Academy of Astronautics; they were close to two thousand, coming from throughout the world to take part in this annual 'High Mass'. Surrounding the wide corridors and many meeting rooms which now replaced the lifting chains of the famous Italian make of car, a scale model under Plexiglas placed on a table with a few leaflets went almost unnoticed. It was about an invitation to send the following message to Pope John-Paul II: 'I encourage the building of the Chapel-House on the Moon—I support the inclusion of the Chapel on the Moon in the program of festivities for Christ's

2000th Jubilee.' To make the operation more effective, the pontifical website address was given: http://www.vatican.va. The drawing which adorned the leaflets and the scale model gave an idea of what this 'Chapel-House' would look like: a series of pointed arches on the lunar surface, the highest one surmounted by a cross.

The project may raise a smile; it no less illustrates one of the characteristics of Christianity (even if shared with other religions) to which I have been alluding at great length: its missionary spirit, its willingness to go and sow the Word of the Gospel and to build churches everywhere that humanity has (or could) set foot. In applying this Christian characteristic to a place where up to the present only a dozen men have effectively left the imprint of their boots, this leaflet also calls forth a definitively universalist or cosmic concept of the salvation brought about and offered by Christ. At the dawn of the third Christian millennium, does the project of the chapel on astral sand not follow, if not naturally, at least logically in the wake of the missions of the Apostles beginning from Jerusalem, and the pilgrimages of the monks of the Columban abbey in the sixth century, and the European missionary zeal of the modern era?

I do not think that the promoters of the project presented in Turin would have envisaged such an evangelisation of the Moon: no one is unaware now about whether the Moon is inhabited, that there is no form of life there, in any case not any who can hear the Good News and receive baptism! Their lunar chapel has nothing in common with the Cross raised by Christopher Columbus on the shore of what was going to become the New World, in order to take possession of it and signify the beginning of evangelisation.

It would rather have something sisterly in common with the crosses and chapels on our mountains. Situated at the boundary between earth and heaven, these structures, these buildings are as much invitations to see, in the effort (physical or technical) which allows them to reach them, an image of the spiritual exercise which can lead to an encounter with the divine, with the Almighty. Is the Moon, in its own way, not the ultimate summit conquered by humanity today?

As far as I know, the project of the chapel on the Moon has not been followed up; but I do not doubt that the question will arise again, at the moment when human constructions have been achieved on the surface of our planet's only natural satellite: the American Antarctic base certainly has its own chaplain! If I have chosen to depict this project, then it is not in order to evaluate its feasibility, but to underline with a dash, before pinpointing it, how modern Space, if I can express myself in this way, has not escaped the religious sphere, that the latter considers it possibly as a new world for (con)quest or that it can impose itself more simply in terms of cultural adaptation.

A Jew in Space

Cape Canaveral, autumn 2002. Ilan Ramon was not the first Jew to be prepared to flirt with the stars on board the American shuttle; Jeff Hoffmann preceded him, several years before already, and even accomplished several missions dedicated to the repair and maintenance of the Hubble space telescope. But if one can believe the media, Ramon, a colonel of Israeli nationality, normally hardly observant, was the first to submit to the Jewish authorities the question of observing the Sabbath while orbiting the earth. Where did he see a problem? You need to know (or remember) that space shuttles like the orbital station move at the speed of approximately 25,000 km per hour and accomplish the range of their orbit around the earth in ninety minutes. In other words, for their occupants, the sun rises about sixteen times every twenty-four hours. Do you follow me? In that case, put yourself in the place of a practising Jewish man and ask yourself how many times in twenty-four hours you ought in theory to observe the Sabbath? The answer is simple: every ten and a half hours, or twice every 'earth day!' This Jewish arithmetical problem appears worthy of figuring in a Talmudic text and in fact it provoked a few upheavals among Florida rabbis, to whom the Israeli astronaut, rather too zealously no doubt, put his problem of conscience. To conclude, he flew on board the shuttle Columbia on the 16th of January 2003, with a dispensation from his religious duties, at least as far as the Sabbath was concerned; for the rest, he had no need to worry: for ages now, NASA has offered kosher menus for its crews.

On the 1st of February, on re-entry into the atmosphere, Columbia exploded, causing the death of Ilan Ramon and his six astronaut companions.

Religion, in its most practical aspects, did not wait for Colonel Ramon in order to have a seat on board space vessels. The prayer of the American astronauts, on board Apollo VIII in orbit around the Moon for Christmas 1968, is a moving illustration. Leaving Cape Kennedy on the 21st of December, Borman, Lovell and Anders, right on Christmas time, accomplished ten revolutions around the Moon, at an altitude of 112 kilometres. Borman, a lay preacher of the Episcopalian parish of League City, formulated the following prayer on that occasion:

> O my God, give us the possibility of seeing your love in the world, in spite of human faults. Give us faith, confidence and goodness, in spite of our ignorance and weakness. Give us knowledge so that we can continue to pray with understanding hearts, and show us what each of us can do to bring about the arrival of universal peace.

In fact, multiple blessings have permeated and still do permeate the space enterprise, in forms as diverse as the cultures to which the astronauts and cosmonauts belong. So I liked hearing Daniel Goldin, when he was the administrator of NASA, salute the memory of Alan Shepard, the first American to have accomplished a Space flight and who died on the 22nd of July 1998, with a vibrant: 'On this final journey, we wish him Godspeed.' To translate Godspeed by 'at the speed of God' would be wrong, since the expression, of mediaeval origin, is the abbreviation of the formula 'May God speed your journey, 'May God be favourable to you in your journey' But is the possible semantic confusion not a happy one?

Seeming to have forgotten Gagarin's word, the Russian astronautic milieu was not to be outdone. At the time of the Andromeda mission, on board the ISS, the International Space Station, at the end of October 2001, at the moment of leaving the astronauts' residence at Baikonor to go to the launch installations of his Soyuz, Claudie Haigneré was seen to be gratified, with her two companions, with a really special blessing pronounced by an Orthodox priest. 'As if, under the pretext of wars of religion', a journalist in the newspaper Liberation of the 23rd of October 2001, protested on the occasion, 'even a peaceful rocket could not be fired without having a priest stand in front of it'. Fortunately the press did not know of the presence of a Catholic priest among the French people who went to Baikonor for the occasion. In fact, that (brief) religious ceremony right in the middle of the most prestigious installations of the former Soviet Union is already no longer revolutionary: a year before, at the time of the departure for the ISS of its first Franco-American crew, a press communiqué announced that 'conforming with the tradition (sic), an Orthodox priest sprinkled the three men with holy water before their departure, and they placed their signature on the door of their hotel room where the giant logo of the ISS was drawn'. The communiqué goes on: 'The rite (sic) also wants cosmonauts to urinate on a wheel of the bus that takes them to the cosmodrome's launch pad, one of the historic places of space conquest which saw Yuri Gagarin leave in 1961 for the first manned flight in space'. The Orthodox rite and the Soviet rite go well together among the cloud-riders.

Another proof of change in the Soviet countries, from July 1995, cosmonauts took two icons of St Anastasia on board the Mir station—they had been formerly and conjointly blessed by Pope John-Paul II and the Orthodox Patriarch Alexis II, as a sign of prayer for peace in the former Yugoslavia. At the moment of Mir's re-entry into the earth's atmosphere, in March 2001, a veteran of Space and hero of the Soviet Union, Guennadi Strekalov, also succumbed to religiosity, since he officially asked pardon of Mir, the defunct station, for not having been able to save her! This slipping from atheist materialism into this form of technological animism makes you wonder . . .

Still on this note of astronautical piety, Europeans are not to be outdone. On the 24th December 1979, after a first aborted attempt nine days beforehand, the CNES got ready to launch the first European Ariane rocket, from the Guyana base of Kourou. Which is to say that tension, among the engineers, was at its height. John Gruau, who presided over the 'review of readiness for launching', the RAL, remembered.

> I said that we had done everything that was humanly achievable, and then I suggested going to place a candle in the Kourou church. I actually think that the SEP placed about eighty [. . .]. Later, we were able to verify that if we omitted suggesting the placing of candles, the launch would fail. That was the case for LO2 and LO5 [. . .]. This gesture finished up becoming a tradition. In the final procedure, the crews would

mention this instruction: go and talk to the inspector general about the candle. Come the first INTELSAT launch in the presence of an American advisor. Fearing ridicule, Frederick d'Allest was annoyed that we were suggesting this business of candles in front of him. However, I insisted, explaining that, if not, the crews would be traumatised. At the end of the review of readiness to launch, profiting from a moment of inattention of the INTELSAT representative who was chatting with Frederick d'Allest, I said over the microphone: 'And then there will be candles'. Later, the NASA advisor came up to me, laughing. 'You know', he confessed, 'back home, we talk about candles, too!'[6]

When I discovered this story, it seemed too good to be true and yet, from information gathered from one of the fathers of Ariane, it is. To apply the dictum 'Help yourself and heaven will help you' in order to reach the celestial vault, well, there's a fine parable[7] for those who love the relationship between science and faith! My informer added that the said custom has not been carried on up till today. On the other hand he told me another anecdote on the same theme.

Ariane was to launch a Japanese satellite. On the predicted date, the Japanese gave us a cool reception: Buddha, they affirmed, had his eyes closed on that day, which, of course, is not a good omen. The RAL did not take notice of the information and decided on the launch. A last minute incident (the detachment of umbilicals, specialists will understand) interrupted the procedure; the launch was delayed for a week to a date revealed as more favourable for the Arianespace clients: then Buddha had his eyes open and the Japanese satellite reached the orbit which had been assigned to it with no problem. How does one say Deo gratias in Japanese?

Jacques Villain, in his parallel history of space conquest, added an ecumenical touch to these anecdotes:

> Europe 1 and 2 were the first space launchers achieved by Europe in the course of the 1960s. There were eleven launches

---

6. France Durand-de Jongh *De la fusée Véronique au lanceur Ariane. (Une Histoire d'hommes 1945–1979* SEP: Société européenne de propulsion (Paris: Stock, 1998), 266–267. LO2 and LO5: acronyms for the second and fifth flights of the *Ariane* rocket.
7. Translators note: parabola—the French word 'parabole' means both.

and all those effected with full launchers were failures. The origin of the Europe setbacks came in great part from a well identified lack of mastery of the task. As in 'L'auberge espagnole'[8] each country brought its propulsion stage, without truly having a whole vision of the system and that in spite of ELDO, (European Launcher Development Organisation), the organisation responsible for the program. Moreover some had been clairvoyant about the organisation of ELDO, highly critical. Thus, in 1963, an article in the American magazine Aviation Week, of good reputation in the space milieu, pointed out that there were three missing positions: that of a Catholic priest, a rabbi, and a pastor so that a bundle of prayers would make the project succeed![9]

But let us return to Colonel Ramon. On what grounds did the rabbis decide to relieve the first Israeli astronaut of his religious duties, respecting the Sabbath not being one of the least? They appear of two kinds. On the one hand, the dangerousness intrinsic to manned flights would dispense the astronaut from this type of observance, with life emergencies prevailing over religious laws. In my opinion, the argument is not relevant: the occupant of a space shuttle or an orbital station runs risks by their very nature (and the tragic outcome of the Columbia mission unfortunately confirmed this; but to speak of emergency is exaggerated, and indeed fallacious. Otherwise, how could astronauts engage in and bring to conclusion scientific experiments with protocols as complex as the rubrics of a religious office? What is more, when confronted with a dangerous situation, how would a person of faith not have the reflex or at least the desire to pray to his God? So it is more honest to recognise that the general conditions of a mission in Space do not seem compatible with certain religious practices, however common they may be on terra firma. It's to this second argument that the rabbis who were questioned rallied; in other words, earthly laws cannot be applied in Space. The simplicity of the argument, I believe, hides a theological abyss.

---

8. Translator's note: meaning 'taking pot luck—you get out what you put in' a reference to the 2002 French Film 'L'auberge espagnole'.
9. Jacques Villain, *Dans les coulisses de la conquéte spatiale* (Toulouse, Cépaduès-Éditions, 2003), 89. Bernard Chabbert, *L'Homme-fusée* (Paris, Arthaud, 1982), 88–389. The author clarifies: 'On that Sunday morning, the church

At the time of the Apollo XI mission, the first lunar liturgy took place—I mean on the surface of the Moon itself. The lunar module had just landed; Neil Armstrong and Buzz Aldrin were having their dinner before making their first sortie. 'Invisible from Earth', Bernard Chabbert relates,

> Aldrin mixed God into his adventure, just as the Conquistadors began their work of brutal conquest, cultural annihilation, and destruction of divine work, by the celebration of a Mass for the work of grace on the virgin sand of a pristine beach; from a small bag he took out a flask containing consecrated wine and a piece of bread [. . .] Aldrin poured the wine into a small chalice which he had placed near the instrument panel; the liquid went down into the container behaving rather like oil because of the weak gravity, then the astronaut read some Bible passages and prayed before receiving communion.[10]

Have we asked ourselves seriously what is happening to our religions and their practices, when they 'go up' into Space? I already put this kind of problem to myself, a few years ago, to the point of asking a brother of my community, a liturgy expert recognised worldwide. So that I did not seem too 'over the top', I played down my question to that of celebrating the Eucharist on board a plane; he replied:

> I have hardly had the experience of truly long plane trips (from Paris to Australia), preventing one from being able to celebrate the same day, before or after (the journey). On the other hand, the trips that I have been able to make do not allow me to appreciate either the stability of planes or whether there would be possibilities for celebrating other than sitting down with one or two neighbours, in all likelihood strangers to the meaning of the celebration. Moreover, in today's world, it seems important to me, even in the absence of a gathering or group of the faithful, that priests are fully aware of the

---

10. Bernard Chabbert, *L'Homme-fusée* (Paris, Arthaud, 1982), 388–389. The author clarifies: 'On that Sunday morning, the church (of the village where Aldrin lived) was packed, and when the pastor reached the Communion he presented to the crowd of faithful a loaf of bread with a corner missing; he did not need to say what had happened to that piece of soft inner and crust, and many present began to weep . . . It was worthy of a Hollywood scenario, and truly symbolic!'

relationship of the priest with the Eucharist. In such a setting, naturally, various equipment problems arise or would arise.

I confess, this response, very reasonable after all, not to say Roman, at the time did not stir me to pursue an investigation in the matter of Eucharist and astronautical liturgy . . . No doubt precisely tomorrow a Catholic priest will climb into a space ship; no doubt also, the authorities in Rome will agree to relieve the first astronaut cleric of his religious obligations, even the most essential. However, at the risk of seeming to belong to those who wonder about the sex of angels while the infidels are at the gates of their Byzantine cenacle, I refuse to consider this liturgical question as secondary or worthy of a science-fiction novel or a space opera (space liturgy!). In fact I see in it an opportunity to measure the terrestrial dimension of our religious beliefs or, to be more modest and honest, of Christian faith and traditions. Even if no priest were ever to leave earth's atmosphere (I would like to add: Please God, no!), I judge it necessary to ask ourselves, even if only once, about the cosmic and astronautic impasse to which a too strict reading of the following liturgical formula could lead: 'Blessed are You, Lord, God of the universe, who give us this bread, fruit of the earth and of the work of human hands . . . this wine, fruit of the vine and of the work of human hands.'

What will happen' the canonist Jean Werck-meister wonders for his part, in the case in which a voyage to Mars, for example, likely to last several years, would oblige us to foresee not only the risk but the likelihood that the members of the crew will not all return to Earth alive? Will sick or dying Catholics be able to receive unction by radio (the Church readily admits that the urbi et orbi benediction is transmitted by radio waves)? Will they have the possibility of carrying the viaticum, just in case? Will it be necessary to train space chaplains, practised in celebrating the sacraments in weightlessness? Will these chaplains be lay or ordained?[11]

These questions, as liturgy historians know, are not unheard of: the squabble over 'Chinese rites' was without doubt one of the most elaborate theological forms in the XVIIth century. But from the

---

11. Jean Werckmeister, 'La conquête de l'espace: questions juridiques et canoniques', in Alexandre Vigne, *Dieu, l'Église et les extraterrestres* (Paris, Albin Michel, 2001), 342.

sixth century, the American Indian and the evangelisation of him posed similar questions: could their millet beer and their manioc flour manifest and bear the real presence of Christ, in the same way as bread and wine? Should we impose the European liturgical calendar on them or adapt it to their own seasonal cycles (at least for the southern hemisphere[12])? In Space, the ditch widens and the question takes on very obviously cosmic dimensions! Rereading Pierre Teilhard de Chardin's famous Mass over the World therefore offers, it seems to me, a judicious preamble to such a reflection. In particular it invites us to define the Christian limits to pantheism, and to all forms of divinisation of the universe; it especially introduces the theological perspective of the cosmic Christ, doubtless as obvious as it is delicate to handle. For the moment, I choose rather to question the idea which has appeared obvious up till now, the very question of the conquest of Space. In other terms, can humanity truly claim to be conquering the universe surrounding it? Are Christians in particular not invited from this very moment, to change their way of regarding Space into a more welcoming rather than missionary, or indeed conquering, attitude?

The Gods'-eye View

The 24th of December 1968. Thanks to the Apollo VIII mission, the first images of Earth, seen from the lunar orbit, appeared on television screens. It was not at all difficult to recognise the dark mass of the continents, the blue surface of the oceans, the blanketing clouds. Our planet was not unknown to us up till then. But, for the first time, we discovered it for what it was in its totality: a blue and white planet ("blue like an orange," wrote Paul Éluard), on a black screen pierced with stars and galaxies. And one of the crew members of Apollo VIII then wondered: 'What would a traveller from another planet think of the Earth?'

---

12. Gui Patin wrote, in September 1463, that in Paris he met 'a man who said that above the Moon, there was a new world, where there were new men, new forests and new seas as fine as in this one. I saw another who said that America and *tota illa terra Australis nobis incognita* was a new world which was not the creation of Adam and that Jesus Christ had not come for their salvation' (*Lettres de Gui Patin*, Paris, 1846, volume 1, 297, quoted in Alexandre Vigne, 'Les extraterrestres du Nouveau Monde', in *Diogéne*, 189 (2000): 70).

The images of Earth, which have since come into the public domain, have become familiar to us . . . even if it means forgetting that they offer the clearest illustrations of its objective to the Apollo space program: to conquer Space in order to affirm the American imperium and to get the better of the Soviets. Is it not the very meaning of the name of the program which has allowed twelve Americans to put their foot on the surface of the Moon and to plant their national flag on it? American patriotism is allied to the Protestant missionary spirit to give meaning to a Promethean enterprise, and in fact to justify it. But that is perhaps not the only possible reading of the overview effect, of the acquisition of what tradition calls the view of the gods.

> 'I know', Ptolemy recognised, 'I am mortal and endure but a day. But when I accompany the serried ranks of the stars in their circular course, my feet no longer touch the earth, I go to the realms of Zeus himself and satisfy myself with ambrosia, like the gods'. In reading Homer, anyone who occupies 'the expanse which separates the earth from the starry sky with Hera's horses, which devour as much space in a moment as can the look of a watching spy embrace the surface of the sea, from a high point, becomes the equal of the gods. He is capable of observing the deeds and gestures of humans, and of their societies, and being amazed, like Poseidon from the peak of Samothrace, 'by the battle and the war' that human beings wage on one another. Man did not wait for the flight of the first airships to rise up above the surface of the Earth, to meet Zeus and surfeit himself on ambrosia, on equal terms with the gods. In imagination, man had for ages prepared for a cosmic journey. Michel de Certeau could therefore remark that 'mediaeval or renaissance painters portrayed the city seen in perspective by an eye that however had never yet existed. At the one time they invented the overview of the city and the panorama that it made possible. That fiction was already changing the mediaeval spectator into a celestial eye. It was creating gods.[13] Anyone who speaks of ascension is therefore not necessarily or uniquely speaking of looking towards the upper world or heavenly realities; take-off quite simply also allows one to see the reality of earth from higher up.

13. Michel de Certeau, *L'invention du quotidien* (Paris, Gallimard, 1990), 140.

Thanks to his exercises in meditation, spiritual elevation or poetry, the person who crawls on the surface of the Earth perhaps does not always acquire the solar eye of a god but experiences the unity at the same time as the harmony of the cosmos. That is the experience lived by Benedict of Nursia, father of monks of the West, and described by Gregory the Great in his Dialogues:

> Benedict was standing at the window, praying to Almighty God. Suddenly, in the depth of night, he saw a light spreading from on high rolling back the darkness of night. It lit up with such splendour that it surpassed the light of day, even though it was shining in darkness. A very marvellous thing followed this contemplation for, as he related afterwards, the whole world, as if gathered under a single ray of sun, was brought before his eyes.

'For the soul who sees the Creator', Gregory then explained, 'the entire creation is small. Although he has seen only a feeble part of the light of the Creator, everything created shrinks before it. In the clarity of interior contemplation, the capacity of the soul becomes enlarged; its expansion into God is such that it becomes superior to the world'.[14] That is also the experience related and analysed by de Certeau, after going to the top of one of the towers of the World Trade Center, which has now disappeared:

> anyone who goes up there exits the mass that carries away and mixes into itself any identity of us as authors or spectators. Icarus above these waters can ignore Daedalus's tricks in endless moving labyrinths. His elevation transfigures him into an onlooker. It puts him at a distance. It mutates the world into a text that you have in front of you, before your eyes, this world which performs sorcery and with which you were 'possessed'. It permits you to read it, to be a solar Eye, to have a god's eye view. The exaltation of a gnostic, radioscopic urge. To be this seeing point only, that is the fiction of knowing.[15]

---

14. Julian of Norwich relates that, in a vision, 'the Creator appeared to her with created matter all complete like a small marble in his hand.'
15. Certeau, *L'invention du quotidie*, 140.

To gain height is also to acquire the power to judge human affairs, with the impartiality advocated by the Stoics and Cynics. In the dialogue written by Lucian The Icaromenippus or the Man who Raised himself above the Clouds), the Cynic philosopher Menippus ridiculed the internal struggles between men, their prayers full of contradictions, this swarming about that excites them and resembles that of an ants nest. Thanks to his mind, Menippus explains, man broadens his knowledge to the dimensions of the cosmos of which he becomes a citizen; he surpasses the human condition at the point where he can denounce the vanity and injustice of inequalities and of social divisions, and the absurdity of war.

The appearing of the lighter, then of the heavier than air, has not diminished the quest, the research, by the human spirit, for a point of view from Sirius. 'True poetry', wrote Goethe after Homer, Menippus, Plato, Seneca, or again Marcus Aurelius, 'is recognised by the fact that, like a profane gospel, it can liberate us from the earthly weights that overwhelm us by giving us interior serenity and exterior pleasure at the same time. Like a balloon, it raises us into the upper regions with the ballast that clings to us, and it causes to appear before our eyes, revealed and untangled, the terrestrial labyrinths that seem inextricable to us'. For his part, Georges Friedmann in La Puissance et la Sagesse, invites us to 'take flight each day'. 'Just one moment that may be brief provided that it is intense', he specifies. 'A spiritual exercise each day . . Make an exit from what goes on and on. Make an effort to get rid of your own passions . . . Become eternal by surpassing yourself'. But the pinnacle of spiritual or mystical experience can also be the supreme temptation for the human mind. The great dream of cartographers, from Anaximander who first wanted to seize the gods' eye view in order to contemplate the Earth, is effectively to bring it back to the dimensions of a sheet of paper, spread out on a table or pinned up on a wall. To see in order to know, certainly, but also to dominate, to possess: 'He who will be master of the sky will be master of the world', affirmed Clement Ader. In the last quarter of the twentieth century, Space offered humanity the chance to fulfil this dream: to acquire the gods' eye view, to conquer the cosmos, to possess heaven. And taking this process as far as getting close to the big bang itself.

23rd of April 1992. The American COBE satellite transmitted the first image of the big bang. It had the look of an egg with blue and pink shades, traces of the minute variations in temperature (of the order of some thirty millionth of a degree) and therefore very weak variations in density of matter, 'foreseen' by the most commonly acknowledged cosmological model today (even if it is regularly criticised). The announcement of the COBE results had an extraordinary impact, not only in the scientific context ('They have found the Holy Grail of cosmology', the physicist Michael Turner explained at the time), but equally among the public. 'Because', stated Kathy Sawyer, a journalist specialising in space affairs, 'the scientific terms are in apparent harmony with the biblical version of creation, such as it has been brought to us, several centuries ago, by scribes ignorant of all relativity, of particle physics and other elements of modern cosmology'. Let us leave aside the concordist temptation that such a harmony can harbour; let us stay with the feeling of satisfaction and even of power that such a discovery can arouse. Stephen Hawking already in the course of his best-seller A Brief History of Time, affirmed:

> If we discover a complete theory, it ought one day to be understandable in the main by everybody, and not just by a handful of scientists. So, all of us, philosophers, scientists, and even people in the street, will be capable of taking part in the discussion on the question of knowing why the universe and we exist. If we find the answer to this question, it will be the ultimate triumph of human reason—at that moment we shall know God's thinking.[16]

George Smoot, an astrophysicist, shows scarcely any more hesitation than Hawking in declaring: 'It is like looking at God.' Patrick J Kiger is almost more modest when he refers to the signature of a black hole observed by the Hubble space telescope: 'It was like having a telephone line to God.' No doubt our contemporaries do not all share the same enthusiasm with regard to astronomy. When questioned about their preference as far as scientific research is concerned, they naturally give the priority to the fields that concern them most directly, in other words health and the environment; astronautics and astronomy generally come far behind, in eighth or even tenth position.

---

16. Stephen W Hawking, *Une brève histoire du temps. Du Big Bang aux trous noirs*, Paris, Flammarion (Champs, 238), 1989), 220.

By contrast it is in this sector that they envisage the most important progress in years or decades to come. It's a way of recognising that, spirit of the pioneers of the Far West or not, Space, revealed by these images and provider of an extraordinary gods' eye view, is effectively perceived at once as a horizon to be conquered and a tool of conquest. And yet, it's still often just a matter of pictures!

The Spirit of Conquest in Question

It is not enough to say that we have entered into a visual culture and indeed a visual civilisation; we must still wonder in what way our relationship with reality is thereby changed. As far as Space is concerned, it is fitting from now on to distinguish our way of perceiving our planet Earth and that of approaching the cosmos, extra atmospheric Space, properly called.

More than two centuries after the flight of the first hot air balloons, one century after the takeoff of heavier than air vessels and more than forty years after Sputnik, we must admit that something has changed in the relationship between humanity and terra firma. Hannah Arendt showed good understanding of that when, as the first astronautic exploits were announced, she wrote: 'Nothing, not even the splitting of the atom, could eclipse the event that the firing of the first Sputnik constituted. It confirms the prophecy engraved on the memorial stone of the Russian scientist Konstantine Tsiolkovski: humanity will not always be riveted to Earth.' A few years later, the biologist Jean Dorst remarked in his turn: 'Man now believes that he possesses enough power to take possession of the vast biological complex that has been his since he has been on earth.'

But, in distancing himself (a little) from Earth, humanity has also acquired a new awareness of the Earth. The astronomer Fred Hoyle prophesied this in about 1948: 'When a photograph of Earth, taken from Space, becomes available, a new idea, more powerful than any other in history, will emerge.' That actually happened about ten years later, with the first manned flights (Vostok in 1961, Voshkod in 1964, Mercury in 1962, Gemini in 1964, then, at the end of the 60s, Apollo). The Gemini missions offered NASA the chance to publish several collections of photographs of Earth from Space, of which the prefaces recall how 'these photographs as well as other experiments conducted with Gemini mark the beginning of a vast increase in humanity's knowledge of Earth and its environment'. However, the most famous views remain without doubt those taken by the crews of Apollo VIII and Apollo XVII, entitled respectively Earthrise (1968) and The Whole Earth (1972). 'The Earth', wrote the astronaut Edgar Mitchell, "is wonderful, harmonious, full of peace, blue with white clouds, and it gives you a profound impression of home, of being, of identity. It is what I prefer to call instant global awareness." And Alfred Sauvy, in the preface to the 1990 edition of L' État de la planéte, can accurately put forward the idea according to which 'it's the Moon walk that is at the origin of the contemporary ecological movement'. Space permits us to carry out a unique experiment on the fragility of Earth and the limitedness of its resources.

In his major work Man and Adaptation to Habitat, René Dubos has underlined this: the human being does not maintain the same type of relations with his habitat as other systems, inanimate or living. He is not content to 'react with' (réagir) his habitat, he is equally capable of responding (répondre) to it, to pick up the distinction proposed, in English, by Dubos. 'Human adaptation', he specifies,

> can rarely be considered as the simple mechanical reaction of our bodies to the physical forces present in our habitat. In fact, man's reactions do not even tend necessarily to surmounting difficulties presented by exterior conditions. Often, they correspond, rather, to a need to express oneself, and imply the use of the habitat in order that the realisation of the Ego may happen there [. . .] Thus, Dubos goes on, human life is the result of the interaction of three distinct kinds of components, namely: the permanent and universal characteristics of human nature which are written into our flesh and blood; the ephemeral situation in which we find ourselves at a given moment; finally, but it is not the least important, our capacity to choose between two possibilities, to decide as a course of action.[17]

'To respond' to habitat and not only 'to react', is of necessity to make a kind of counterpart of it, to put some distance with regard to it, whether to master it, or to make a partner of it. Animism, which

---

17. R Dubos, *L'homme et l'adaptation au milieu* (Paris: Payot, 1973), 8.

establishes a kind of alliance between nature and humanity and tries to explain natural phenomena and human activity in the same way and by the same laws (subjective, conscious and projective), is an example of partnership. The scientific achievements and techniques of the modern West offer an example of mastery of habitat, or, to be more exact, of habitats. Of course, according to each case, the relationship with nature is totally different: attachment and partnership in the first (Mitwelt, Germans say, to designate the-world-with), detachment in the second (at best, Umwelt in the precise sense of world-around, environment). Martin Heidegger in 1958, described this last process in the following terms: 'Nature, technically able to be mastered by science and the natural nature of the human sojourn, habitual and historically determined at the one time, take their distance like two foreign domains and grow apart from each other at an ever more crazy pace.'

Attachment and detachment: the bond of humanity to its mother Earth can no longer from now on be reduced to conquest alone. Without doubt, in techniques of satellite observation, the part left to the procedures of 'virtualisation' is sufficiently great to recall how these techniques are very much the heirs of the slogan of the modern West: to become master and possessor of nature. However, even if the pictures in Spot'Art sometimes appear too beautiful to be true, they none the less urge and invite us to protect and manage our planet better, to consider it as 'our' environment and not just any old world among others. The gods' eye view is not only that of Apollo, the conquering warrior, but also that of Gaia, nourishing and maternal goddess. But we know all too well how heavy is the task which consists in retying the bonds with the Earth after they have been in part untied by our technology, our science and even our modern cultures.

At this point I can hear a remark, or indeed an objection: this relativisation of the conquering nature of Space is hardly surprising as far as observation, study, understanding of Earth is concerned: the world in question is not quite unknown! If not, why would we complain sometimes about the piercing eye of the voyeur satellites? Is it possible to say as much about the other side of the space enterprise, the one that directs the interests and efforts of humanity towards regions that it does not yet know, and which, because of that, do not directly concern its own identity? The spirit of conquest has not yet finished blowing over the space enterprise, to the point where the putting on guard of Bartholomew de Las Casas can still be taken seriously:

> This term or word conquest, as far as the Indies discovered or yet to be discovered goes, is tyrannical, Mohammedan, abusive, iniquitous and infernal . For there could not be any wars against the Moors anywhere in the Indies, as in Africa, nor against the Turks and heretics who possess our lands, persecute Christians and try to destroy our holy faith: it is only a matter of preaching the Gospel of Christ there, and of propagating the Christian religion there and of converting souls there. Which requires, not armed conquest, but the persuasion of sweet, divine words, and the exemplary works of a holy life. Consequently, there is no need at all for those damned warnings which have been made until now, and the undertaking in the Indies should not be called conquest, but preaching of the faith, salvific conversion of those infidels, who are ready to receive Jesus Christ without delay as universal creator, and His Majesty as a providential and Catholic sovereign. Such is the authentic Christian name of this Indies enterprise.[18]

From now on, ought we not introduce into the space enterprise that has turned towards extra-atmospheric Space the dialectic attach/detach, tie/untie, in brief the process of distancing which is what it is about on the topic of Earth? Arguments in favour of such an evolution in mentality do not stem only from moral doctrine, but equally from a simple fact: if, for centuries, indeed millennia, humanity has essentially imagined Space (as it used to 'imagine' the maps of countries on earth before being able to take flight), the scientific revolution of Modern Times, and in first place that of Copernicus and Galileo, has not furnished much more reality, but pictures more than anything else! Apart from meteorites which regularly fall on our heads, the rocks brought back from the surface of the Moon, and of course, the Earth itself, we do not possess anything else concrete and tangible from Space: not much to play at conqueror with! From now on, would it not be better to be prepared to consider Space as a counterpart, a possible partner?

---

18. Bartolomé De Las Casas, *Memorial de remedios*, 1542, quoted in Marcel Bataillon and André Saint-Lu, *Las Casas et la défense des Indiens* (Paris: Julliard 1971), 193–194.

Contributors

Jacques Arnould, theologian and historian of sciences, is the Ethics Adviser for the French Space Agency (CNES). He has published with ATF Press, *God versus Darwin* (2009), *Dieu, le jour d'après* (2015) and *God, the Moon, and the Astronaut* (2016).

Balachandar Baskaran, Sissi Enestam, Femi Ishola, Dawoon Jung, Paul Kelly, Dong Weihua, Master of Space Studies Participants - International Space University, Illkirch-Graffenstaden

CPSIA information can be obtained
at www.ICGtesting.com
Printed in the USA
FFOW02n1344150316
22363FF

9 781925 309126